Christmas as I knew it in Trinidad

NALINI BISSAMBHAR - SANKAR

FOREWORD

Christmas in Trinidad and Tobago is a **unified** holiday celebrated by people of **all** races and religions. The diversity of Christmas in Trinidad and Tobago is experienced through food, music and traditions influenced by our ancestors who made our special little islands their home, so may years ago. It was only after preparing the glossary for this book that I realized how diverse our Christmas traditions really were. Our food and music at Christmas time has been richly influenced by the native Amerindians, the Spanish, English, Africans, Chinese and East Indians. This makes Christmas in Trinidad and Tobago unique in so many ways and as the saying goes :

"Trini Christmas is truly the Best"

DEDICATION

I dedicate this book to my parents

Jeewanlal Buzzy Bissambhar
&
Nargis Besai-Bissambhar

who managed to make our Christmases magical and memorable
no matter if they had a little or a lot.

My brothers, sister and I remain four humble hearts to this day because of their
imaginative spirit and unconditional love.

Tock tock tock goes the little tin clicker toy that I just got from my school's Christmas treat!

It is the last day of school and also the beginning of my Christmas holidays.

Today at school we got in line to see Santa Claus who gave me a brown paper bag filled with goodies such as an apple, popcorn, balloon, toffee and the all time favorite tock tock toy*.

The scent of the apple combined with the brown paper bag will be a reminiscence of Christmas in Trinidad for the rest of my life!

TOCK TOCK TOY OR TIN LITHO CLICKER TOY

I get home and already the Christmas preparations have begun!

New curtains are up and new vinyl table cloths with a pretty poinsettia flower print have been spread on the table. The new vinyl scent mixed with that of fresh paint adds to the excitement of the holiday!

We have already put up our plastic Christmas tree and decorated it with colorful Christmas lights and shiny tinsel! We place wrapped empty boxes under the tree as decorations but occasionally check to see if presents have magically appeared in them!

POINSETTIA FLOWER

The kitchen is the busiest place!

Daddy is sticking cloves in the ham getting it ready for the oven, while mummy is kneading the dough for our homemade bread.

Aunty is making potato and chicken liver stuffing which is a customary side dish that goes with bread and ham.

Grandma is mixing the batter for her famous sponge cake and letting the children lick the spoon after she puts the mixture in the baking dish.

The women have also made black cake*, cassava pone* and sweet bread* as Christmas desserts to share among our family and neighbors who stop by.

The house smells heavenly with the mixed scent of baked goods in the air.

HOT BREAD AND HAM COMING OUT THE OVEN

While the others are busy, uncle takes us for a drive through the village so we can see all the beautifully lit Christmas trees in everyone's gallery*.

We have a blast counting them and then return home to find daddy and his friends playing sweet parang* music on their guitars and shak-shak maracas* .

Throughout the rest of the night friends and neighbors stop by bringing us more goodies. It is customary during the holidays that your table is always prepared so friends and family can stop by to join in your holiday cheer.

MUSICAL INSTRUMENT: SHAK-SHAK OR MARACAS

By now the women are done with the baking and have begun preparing traditional Christmas drinks such as sorrel* , ginger beer* and punch ah creama*.

Our next door neighbor has sent us pastelles* over the fence and mummy in turn has given her a small basket filled with our home made treats.

Our other neighbor has sent us bottles of freshly made sorrel drink made from the sorrel fruit that she has picked from her own garden. Mummy gives her some of ours and they joke about whose is better.

It is getting late and the children are tired but still waiting to see if they would get a glimpse of Santa Claus.

We leave Santa a glass of milk and a plate of cookies and reluctantly head to bed.

SORREL DRINK

On Christmas morning , my eyes shoot open wide with excitement and expectation!

I awaken my siblings and we race to the Christmas tree where we are not at all disappointed!

Santa had been there!

The cookies were eaten, the milk had been drank and most importantly there was a beautifully wrapped present with each of our names written on it!

At that time the adults are up and have come looking to see what the commotion is about!

They lovingly wish us a merry Christmas and we hurriedly open our presents.

The boys get cars and trains and my sister and I get two beautiful baby dolls. Hers has a pink dress and mines a blue.

We are so happy and thankful. Santa has been good to us!

MY SISTER AND I

WITH OUR DOLLS THAT SANTA GOT US.

Daddy serves us our Christmas breakfast consisting of homemade bread and ham and a glass of sorrel. How delicious it tastes!

By this time mummy, grandma and aunty have begun preparing our Christmas day lunch which will consist of various Trinidadian dishes.

I watch as my mama expertly rolls out roti* that mummy has filled with dhal*. The women work in unison and before we know it they are done making delicious dhalpuri roti*.

Daddy is also busy cooking his special recipe fried rice and baked chicken.

He is also cooking various curried and stewed meats.

The mixed smell of the various dishes being prepared creates a stir in my stomach and I head into the kitchen for a snack.

DHALPURI ROTI WITH CURRIED MEAT

The best part about Christmas in Trinidad is having so many yummy snacks readily available.

There is so much goodies to eat I cannot decide which to have!

In addition to all the homemade baked goods, there is an abundance of treats such as chocolates, candies, apples, grapes, wafers and not forgetting extra special things to drink like Peardrax* and Malta*

I end up grabbing a hand full of toffees and hurry off to play with my toys.

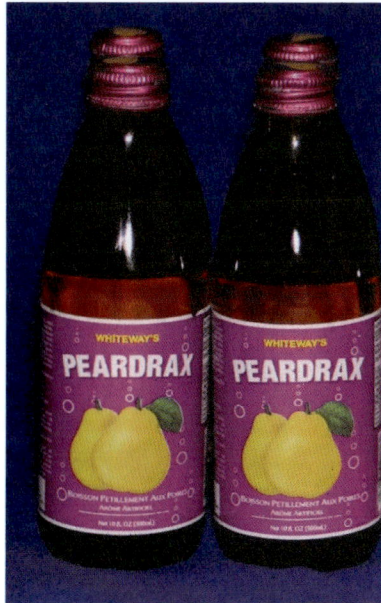

PEARDRAX PEAR DRINK

Mummy sends us to put on our new clothes and I feel very special in the beautiful dress my grandmother has sewn for me as my Christmas gift from her!

It is now Christmas afternoon and our home is filled with family, friends, music and lots of laughter.

Food, snacks and drinks are plentiful. So is the laughter of children and adults as everyone is in their jolliest mood.

Daddy brings out his guitar and shak-shak maracas and they start singing parang songs again .

Soon everyone is singing along and dancing to the intoxicating beat.

Parang   Parang   Parang

As night approaches we turn on the lights on our beautiful, colorful Christmas tree and my heart is filled with awe at its dazzling beauty.

I grab my final snack of the night, a whole apple and happily bite into it. Apples do not grow here in Trinidad so it is an extra special treat at Christmas time to me!

I stand in our front porch, eating my juicy apple and look up and down the street.

I can hear parang music playing everywhere and see colorful lights twinkling from every house.

I close my eyes and take a mental picture which still lives in my memory today as Christmas as I knew it in Trinidad......

A True TRINI LOVES
Sorrel • Black Cake
TRINI CHRISTMAS

Trini Christmas is the Best!

GLOSSARY

TOCK TOCK OR TIN LITHO CLICKER TOY – PAGE 4 - A tin toy, or tin lithograph toy, is a mechanical toy made out of tinplate and colorfully painted to resemble primarily a character or vehicle. Originated in Germany in the early 1850's.

BLACK CAKE – PAGE 8 - Also known as fruit cake or rum cake .Traditionally made at Christmas time in Trinidad and Tobago with fruits soaked in dark rum or red wine.

CASSAVA PONE – PAGE 8 – Sweet sticky dessert made with cassava or yucca, coconut, pumpkin, flour and butter . Originally introduced by the early Amerindian settlers of Trinidad and Tobago.

SWEET BREAD – PAGE 8 – A cake like dessert bread made with coconut and fruit.

GALLERY – PAGE 10 – The front porch or verandah of a house in Trinidad and Tobago is sometimes referred to as the "gallery"

PARANG – PAGE 10 - Folk music originating from Trinidad and Tobago which was brought to the island by Venezuelan migrants who were primarily of Amerindian, Spanish and African heritage, something which is strongly reflected in the music itself. The word is derived from two Spanish words: *parranda*, meaning "a spree or fête", and *parar* meaning "to stop".In the past, it was traditional for parang serenaders to pay nocturnal visits to the homes of family and friends, where part of the fun was waking the inhabitants of the household from their beds. Today, parang is especially vibrant in Trinidad and Tobago communities such as Paramin, Lopinot and Arima during the Christmas season.

SHAK- SHAK OR MARACAS – PAGE 10 - The shak-shak (or *chak-chak*) is a kind of Antillean musical instrument, similar to the maracas or shakers. They are played in Barbados, Grenada, Montserrat, Trinidad and elsewhere in the Caribbean. They are typically used by Montserratian string bands, the Barbadian Crop Over bands and in Trinidadian Parang bands.

SORREL – PAGE 12 – The scientific name for the plant we refer to as sorrel is actually the Roselle (Hibiscus Sabdariffa) It is a species of Hibiscus native to west Africa. In the Caribbean, the sorrel drink is made from sepals of the roselle. It has been traced back to Jamaica in the 1600's where it was introduced by the Akan slaves who were bought to the Caribbean from Africa.. It is prepared by boiling dried sepals and calyces of the Sorrel plant in water for 8 to 10 minutes (or until the water turns red), then adding sugar. It is often served chilled. The sorrel drink is also popular in Saint Kitts and Nevis, Guyana, Antiqua, Barbados, St. Lucia, Dominica, Grenada and Trinidad and Tobago.

PUNCH AH CREAMA – PAGE 12 – The drink also known as Ponche Crema or Ponce de Crema is a Trinidadian and Venezuelan based cream liqueur. Recipes vary depending on the region, but main ingredients typically include milk, eggs, sugar, rum and other minor ingredients. Ponce de Crema is a beverage traditionally served in Venezuela and neighboring Trinidad and Tobago during Christmas time, much as eggnog is in the United States.

PASTELLE – PAGE 12 – Trinidadian pastelles are small meat-filled cornmeal pies stuffed with meat, fish or vegetables seasoned with fresh herbs and flavoured with raisins, olives and capers. They are wrapped and steamed in a banana leaf. They are traditionally prepared and eaten during the Christmas season. It is believed that they were introduced by Spanish colonizers who ruled between the late 15th and early 18th centuries.

ROTI – PAGE 16 - Roti is generally an Indian flat bread made from flour and cooked on a heated flat metal over an open fire. Roti is eaten widely across the West Indies, especially in countries with large Indo-Caribbean populations such as Trinidad and Tobago. Originally brought to the islands by indentured laborers from South Asia, roti has become a popular staple in the culturally rich cuisines of Trinidad and Tobago, Guyana and Jamaica. In the West Indies, roti is commonly eaten as an accompaniment to various curries and stews. The traditional way of eating roti, is to break the roti by hand, using it to sop up sauce and pieces of meat from the curry. However, in the West Indies, the term roti may refer to both the flat-bread(roti) its self as well as the more popular street food item, in which the roti is folded around a savory filling in the form of a wrap.

DHAL – PAGE 16 – Split peas.

DHALPURI ROTI – PAGE 16 – Roti as per definition above. However the dough is first filled with boiled and ground split peas mixed with spices and seasonings, which is then rolled out and cooked on a flat metal over an open fire.

PEARDRAX – PAGE 18 – Whiteway's Peardrax is a pear flavored fizzy soft drink popular in Trinidad and Tobago. It originated in the United Kingdom, and was first manufactured by Whiteway's, a now-defunct cider company founded in the United Kingdom during the 19th century. As of 2007 it is bottled and distributed only by Pepsi-Cola Trinidad Bottling Company, under license since 2004.

MALTA – PAGE 18 - Malta is a lightly carbonated malt beverage, brewed from barley, hops, and water much like beer , however, Malta is non-alcoholic. Malta is brewed in the Caribbean and can be purchased in areas with substantial Caribbean populations. Malta originated in Germany as Malzbier ("malt beer") in the 1950's.

SORREL RECIPE

Ingredients:

1 cup dried or fresh sorrel sepals
10 cups water
1 cup sugar
Orange peel
2 tbsp grated ginger
2 cinnamon sticks
1 tbsp cloves

Procedure:

Bring water to boil
Reduce heat and add ginger, orange, cinnamon, glove and sorrel
Allow to simmer for 10 – 15 minutes
Remove from heat and steep for 6 – 12 hours
Add sugar and strain
Refrigerate and serve chilled

CHILLED SORREL DRINK

HOME MADE HOPS BREAD RECIPE

Ingredients:

4 cups flour (or 3¾ cups of flour and ¼ cup of whole wheat)
1 ½ tbsp.. dry instant yeast
2 tsp sugar
1 ¼ cups water
1 tsp salt

Procedure:

Sift flour in a medium sized bowl. Add sugar, yeast, and salt. Mix the dry ingredients well.

Form a well in the middle of the ingredients and pour the water all at once. Mix with a fork thoroughly before kneading.

Knead for 8 to 10 minutes adding flour if necessary to make a medium stiff dough.

Grease the bowl and the top of the dough. Cover and allow the dough to rise for about 25 minutes.

Punch down the dough and form into balls. Place the balls on a grease tray and cover with a damp cloth, and allow to rise for about 1 hour or until it double in size.

Bake in a preheated oven 400°F for 20 minutes.

Makes 9 – 10 hops bread.

HOME MADE HOPS BREAD

BLACK CAKE RECIPE

FOR THE CAKE
1 lb unsalted butter
1 lb sugar
8 eggs
1 tsp lemon essence
2 tsp lime rind
2 tsp almond essence
2 tsp vanilla
1 lb all-purpose flour
4 tsp baking powder
2 tsp mixed spice
1/2 tsp grated nutmeg

FRUIT MIXTURE
1 lb pitted prunes
1 lb raisins
1 lb currants
1 bottle cherry brandy
1 bottle rum

THE BROWNING
1 lb brown sugar
1/2 cup boiling hot water

Procedure on Page 32

BLACK CAKE RECIPE CONTINUED

PROCEDURE:

Three days before:

Chop all the fruits and place in a large bowl. Pour cherry brandy and rum and leave in a cool corner, covered, so that it can soak up the alcohol. 3 days before is accepted but the longer you leave it the better! One day should be minimum though!

Baking day – Blend Fruits:

Pour the soaked fruit and remaining juices into a blender and blend until thick and chunky.

Prepare The Browning:

Burn the sugar until it has caramelized and add hot water gradually. Let this mixture cool.

1. Preheat oven to 275F
2. Cream the butter and sugar.
3. Add eggs one at a time, mixing in
4. Add lemon zest, almond essence and vanilla
5. Mix and sift flour, baking powder, mixed spice and nutmeg.
6. Gradually add sifted ingredients to creamed mixture
7. Mix in fruit base and 'browning' prepared earlier
8. Pour batter into greased baking dishes
9. Bake for 3 hours
10. Once removed from the oven soak with equal portions of rum to your liking

A SLICE OF BLACK CAKE

FESTIVALS OF TRINIDAD AND TOBAGO
By
Nalini Bissambhar – Sankar

BOOK 1 – DIVALI AS I KNEW IT IN TRINIDAD
BOOK 2 – CHRISTMAS AS I KNEW IT IN TRINIDAD

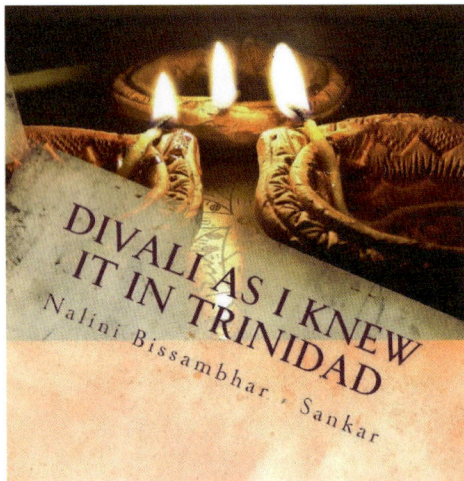

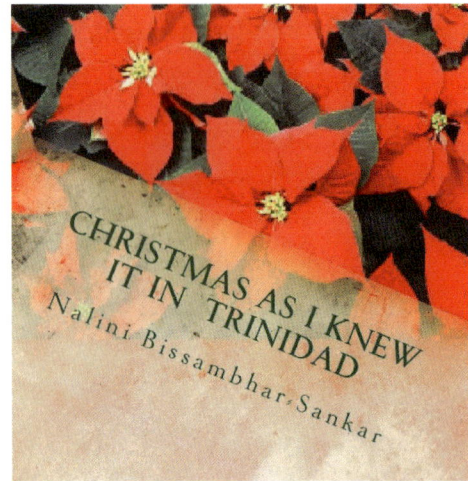

Printed in Great Britain
by Amazon